Ask Jackie

Water Bath Canning

ISBN: 978-0-9860152-7-4

Backwoods Home Magazine
PO Box 712
Gold Beach, Oregon 97444
www.backwoodshome.com

Edited by Jessie Denning, Julia Denning, Haley Kessel, Connie Sayler, Lisa Nourse, Rhoda Denning, and Ilene Duffy
Cover art by Don Childers
Illustrations by Don Childers, Jessie Denning, and John Dean

Contents

Introduction

Water bath canning, or boiling water bath canning as it's often called, is the most simple method of canning. It's basically placing your filled jars of food into very hot water, covering the jars, and processing the jars for a certain length of time. It's quick and easy, but it is limited. Water bath canning should only be used to can fruits, jams, jellies, preserves, and pickles, as they are high-acid foods. Bacteria that could damage these foods are killed at boiling water temperature.

Unfortunately, low-acid foods such as vegetables, meats, and mixtures of the two, can contain bacteria and toxins that are not killed at boiling water temperature, no matter how long the jars of food are held in the boiling water bath canner. Therefore, these foods must be pressure canned.

Most of the questions in this book deal with some aspect of water bath canning, but there could be a couple that deal with pressure canning.

Water bath canning foods is a great starting point for beginners to learn to can a wide array of tasty foods, eventually building up their confidence and desire to go on to pressure canning.

In this book I answer questions on all aspects of water bath processing food, including: jams, jellies, preserves, fruit, and pickles. Have fun reading. I hope I've answered many of your own questions along the way.

— Jackie Clay

Jellies

Sealing jars

I just recently took an interest in making jellies, jams, and chutneys. I primarily do this around the holiday season for gifts. However, after reading your article on canning, I am concerned that I am not doing this right. I was told by my mother that all I would need to do is to sterilize the jars and then put my hot mixture into the jars and let them seal, so this is what I have been doing, and they have been sealing. She never indicated to me that I should then put the filled jars back in for more processing time.

Can you tell me how long the jams, etc. will be good for by the process I have been doing? I have made many jars already and hope that I can still use these for the holidays at least. My mom swears that they will keep for years with this process, also. I would appreciate it if you could please shed some light on this.

Jolee

Bottom line: always listen to your mother. Seriously, she is right. However, as some people in the past have put up big batches of jams, jellies, preserves, etc., and the batch has cooled down some while the entire batch was put into jars, the result was that some jars did not seal properly. Some jars molded and fermented so canning companies and home economists now often recommend processing smaller batches and processing many recipes with a water bath canner for a short time. This ensures the jars seal well and that the food remains hot enough to kill any molds and bacteria that could damage the food in storage.

Follow your recipe and if you are happy with it, keep up the good work. Some of my recipes require only filling hot, sterilized jars with a high-acid food (jam, pickle, jelly, etc.) and sealing with a hot lid and ring. Others advise a hot water bath processing time (often only five or ten minutes) to ensure sealing. I follow the recipe. It's usually when you improvise by doubling a recipe or otherwise altering it that you find yourself in trouble.

I have unprocessed jars of relish, jelly, etc. that are 10 or more years old, and still of excellent quality.

Putting wax on jelly

Hello. It's my first time ever making jam and I used metal-sealed lids and did the hot water bath. But, everyone told me maybe I should put wax just in case, so I put wax on the hot jelly and sealed it. Then I put it in the hot water bath. Is that okay? Or will it all be ruined? One tipped over too, with the wax.

Natalie

You don't need to use wax when you can jelly with regular canning jars and two-piece lids, using the hot water bath. I think your jelly will be alright. When wax is poured on top of hot jelly, it settles to the top and hardens. I've used it in past times, when it was common practice to use "odd" jars as jelly jars and top the jelly off with wax. Unfortunately, several times mice would nibble through the wax to get at the jelly. This was not pleasant. So I began saving the odd jar lids to cap the wax-covered jelly. This was a pain, as you cannot imagine how many different lids and screw rings there are on these jars.

Now I simply use common pint and half-pint canning jars and process the filled jars in a hot water bath to ensure sealing. Simple, quick, and painless.

When you grow a good crop, put up all you can

I would like to know how long my home canned beach plum jelly can safely be kept on the shelf?

Pam Hall

How about forever? Honestly, Pam, most all home canned food, especially jams and jellies, can remain wholesome and great tasting for years and years on your pantry shelves. This is the reason that when I have a bounty of a certain food, I can all I can possibly put up, because in some years some things just don't make a crop. This allows you to build up a solid storage pantry. Some folks tell me, "Oh, I only canned 20 pints of green beans and gave away the rest. We only eat a few jars every year, anyway."

Phooey! Maybe next year the beans will freeze, be eaten by pests, or whatever. When I have the opportunity, I put up all I can.

Pectin

What is apple pectin? I know it is used in canning but how does it work? Under what circumstances and with what foods is it necessary in canning? I have also heard it can be helpful with arthritis/joint health and maintaining colon health. Are there other uses for it?

How does one obtain apple pectin from apples if there is no store? In other words, how did our great-grandmothers obtain, store, and use it? Can you get pectin from other fruits than apples? I think I have heard that grapes might have it — is that correct? I seem to recall my mom saying that she didn't need to add pectin to her grape jelly because it already had it.

E. R.

Pectin is a naturally occurring substance found in many fruits that causes jelly and jam to jell. We often use it because if you do not use it in jams or jellies made from lower pectin fruits, you must mix the juice/purée and sugar, then slowly boil down the jam/jelly until the jelling point is reached; the product will solidify into jelly or jam and not remain a syrup. The only things you use pectin for in most canning is in jams and jelly. Preserves have enough fruit and sugar to set up without pectin added. The reason most modern home canners use pectin in their jams and jellies is that from a smaller amount of juice/purée, mixed with sugar, you'll end up with more end product than if you just boil the sugar and juice/purée down until it jells.

To obtain apple pectin from apples, simply boil the skins and apple cores and even small immature green apples, sliced into thin slices. To a pound of this, add 1 pint of water. Simmer for 15 minutes. Use cheesecloth to strain off the juice. You may return the pulp to the kettle and again add a pint of water and simmer for another 15 minutes. Let this stand 10 minutes, then strain off the juice; do not squeeze the cheesecloth bag. Four cups of homemade pectin is used in place of ½ bottle of liquid pectin in most recipes.

Yes, grapes do have pectin, as do quinces and several other fruits in lesser degrees. But to make your own pectin, apples really are the best.

Put up jelly in small batches for success

I am confused about all the different things I have read about making jelly (crabapple). Boil it too long and the pectin can be ruined and it is runny. Don't boil it enough, or add too much sugar, and it is runny. Boil it too long and it is gummy.

The spoon test never seems to work for me. I have to boil it for hours to make it glob off of the spoon like that. So I used a thermometer and boiled it to "8 degrees above boiling point in your area" according to "Joy of Cooking," which is 210 degrees. It hovered at 208 for about an hour, then finally hit 210. I put it in the jars and it is runny. Is there a more foolproof way to tell when to put it in the jars without using commercial pectin?

Tania Dibbs, Colorado

I think you are making too large a batch of jelly at a time. Jelly is one thing that must be put up in smaller batches for success. Crabapples are high in pectin, so are quite easy to get the jelly to jell. And yes, the spoon test does work, if the jelly is jelled properly. Here's a simple crabapple jelly recipe you might like to try.

Chop or quarter crabapples (about 3 pounds) and add 1 cup water to each heaped quart of crabapples in large kettle. Cover and simmer fruit until quite soft. Strain through a damp jelly bag or cheesecloth bag overnight.

4 cups crabapple juice
4 cups sugar

Put the crabapple juice in a large kettle and add sugar. Bring to a boil over high heat, stirring constantly. Cook to jelling point, where the jelly slides off a cool spoon in a sheet instead of drips. The spoon must be cool and not damp from washing it. When this point is reached, turn off the heat and quickly ladle the jelly into hot half-pint or pint jars to within ¼ inch of the top of the jar. Process the jelly in a water bath canner for 10 minutes.

This makes about six half-pint jars. If you want more jelly, simply make more juice. You can make lots of juice, keeping the same proportions. Then make one batch of jelly at a time using the above recipe. Do not double or triple the recipe to save time. You'll often have failures.

Homemade grape jelly and juice

My mother used to make homemade grape jelly and grape juice. She recently passed away and I do not know where her recipes are for these items. I do know that she used Sure-Jell in her jelly and she used so many cups of sugar to so many cups of juice, cooking for so long. She also used to put wax on top of the jelly before putting on the lid.

Would appreciate it if you could supply me with any recipes or at least direct me to where I might obtain them. Your consideration will be appreciated.

Linda Linderman, Florida

My grandmothers and mother also used to make lots of homemade grape jelly and grape juice. We even used to have a large grape arbor (you seldom see those anymore, which is too bad) in our side yard, from which baskets and baskets of succulent, sweet grapes were harvested every fall. Grape jelly and grape juice are very easy to make at home. You can get a box of Sure-Jell at the grocery; inside you'll find a very good list of common jelly and jam recipes. Here are the basics for both juice and jelly. I'm sure it will be just about what your mother made. Grape juice:

> Stem and wash ripe grapes. Cover them with water and heat slowly. Do not boil hard; only simmer. Cook slowly until grapes are very soft, then strain through a bag as you would for jelly. Do not press, or the juice will be cloudy instead of clear. To each quart of juice, add half a cup of sugar (or to taste). Mix well. Pour into clean jars to within half an inch of the top. Wipe rim of jar clean and place hot, previously boiled lid on jar and screw down ring firmly tight. Process jars for 15

> minutes in a water bath canner, counting from the time that the canner comes to a full rolling boil. Be sure that the water covers the jars by at least one inch.

As well as using a jelling agent such as Sure-Jell, you can simply add juice and sugar and boil it until it reaches the jelling point — when a teaspoon full of the hot jelly will slide off a spoon in a sheet, not drip off. Here's such a recipe. Grape jelly:

> Extract grape juice as above. Measure and bring to a boil in a very large kettle. For each cup of juice, add three quarters of a cup of sugar. Boil hard to jelly stage. Pour into jars, seal, and water bath for 10 minutes.

As your mother did, I used to use the old method of pouring melted paraffin on top of the jelly or to coat the top of the jar and lid with it. As we used to use "odd" jars for jellies, we usually used the paraffin to seal the jelly. This was okay, but really not so hot. Any movement would often crack the seal loose, resulting in leaking jelly or moldy jelly. The mold was completely harmless, but ugly. It can be spooned off, but no one feels like eating the jelly after seeing the mold. Also, mice would nibble through the wax and sample the jellies which was unhealthy and very unappetizing, especially when they left little rodent "presents" on top of the wax.

Today, I use standard pint and half-pint jars with new lids. These are sealed in a water bath canner as above. No leaks. No mold. No mice. Much more economical as you don't lose processed food. And because our home canned jams and jellies are so good, who wants to lose even one jar?

Wild grape jelly

I was at a craft show a couple of years ago, and tried some homemade jelly. The seller said it was made from the small wild grapes in her yard. She called them Fox grapes. Could you let me know if anyone has a recipe they would like to share? My wild grape vines are full of grapes this year and I would like to make them into jelly. She said they are also used in wine.

Jo Edwards

Lucky you! There is no finer jelly than wild grape. You can find a simple recipe for grape jelly inside any powdered pectin product, such as Sure-Jell, at your grocery store. Or you can make your jelly the old-fashioned way with just grape juice and sugar.

To do this, place grapes in a large kettle and add about ¼ cup of water per pound (or just enough water to get the grapes cooking without scorching them). Simmer them, covered, until they are tender. Then crush them with a potato masher. For large batches, you may want to invest in a juicer, such as a Mehu-Maija, which extracts juice simply from steaming the grapes. I've never been able to afford one, so I crush, then pour the grapes/juice through a jelly bag which is simply a square of doubled old white sheet. Tie the bag and its contents up securely over a counter with a large glass or stainless steel bowl underneath to catch the juice.

Don't try to squeeze the bag to get more juice. This results in a cloudy jelly instead of a jewel-like, sparkling jar of purple.

Let the bag hang overnight. The next day, for each cup of juice, add a cup of sugar. Place this in a large stainless steel kettle to allow for the rolling boil to rise high in the kettle without boiling over. Heat over high heat, stirring almost constantly until the jelly will slide off a cool teaspoon in a sheet when tilted upright. If it runs off in drips it is not ready.

When the jelly will sheet, immediately ladle into hot, sterilized jars to within half an inch of the top, wipe the rim of the jar clean and quickly place a hot, previously boiled lid on and screw down the ring firmly tight. Place jars in a hot water bath for ten minutes.

Apple jelly

I have tried making apple jelly from apple juice. I always follow the instructions exactly, but it always seems not to set up. Can you give me a good recipe for this or tell me what I am doing wrong? We love apple jelly and I love to can my own vegetables.

Reneé Hoover

First of all, be sure your apple juice is 100% apple juice. I would guess that you perhaps got an apple juice drink, which includes sugar and water to "thin" it down. That would certainly account for batches that didn't turn out. I use the recipe that comes in the Sure-Jell box. It's easy, quick, and has always worked for me.

Chokeberry jelly

I've been cruising the net and came across an article by you about canning. You mention chokecherry jelly. I'd sure like to have that recipe. My last batch came out as syrup. (Still good, but too thin). Can you help?

Richard & Georgia Trathen

Sometimes my jelly comes out too thin, too. I get into a hurry and mess up. We still love it, as I use it on pancakes, as syrup — gourmet syrup. So, with jelly, there is no failure. Okay, you say, I want jelly that jells. The most often-made mistakes are making too large a batch at one time (my usual reason for failing to jell) or not following the recipe exactly. This is a must-do for jellies and jams.

Chokecherry jelly

When I was young, my parents and siblings would come to Colorado to visit Grandma and Gramps. I remember her fresh baked bread, green chili, and always chokecherry jelly.

We have three bushes on our property. Jackie, why didn't I ask Grandma for her recipe? I was a lot younger then and too busy eating and not paying attention. It must be simple but I still don't have the recipe for this wonderful berry. Grandma and Mom are gone now.

I have attempted making it a couple of times, but I don't remember what berry recipe I used. The second time was a failure. It did not settle, so we used it as a syrup.

Cordelia Webb, Colorado

Chokecherry jelly is one of our favorites. We love the intense cherry flavor, and the beautiful, glistening, purplish-red color that makes a jar of jelly look like a rare gem, plus the fact that you can find chokecherries in so many states. We picked them in New Mexico, Michigan, Montana, and

Wyoming. There are several recipes, but here's a simple good one:

Chokecherry jelly:

Place about 2 quarts of freshly picked chokecherries into a large kettle with 3 cups of water. Simmer the cherries, then mash them with a potato masher or large spoon. Here I let the soft cherries cool, then I really squish them by hand. This releases a lot of color and flavor. It also turns your hands purple. But this is quite temporary.

Then hang the cherry pulp in a jelly bag over a large bowl overnight to drip. You will need 3 cups of chokecherry juice.

3 cups chokecherry juice
6½ cups sugar
1 bottle liquid fruit pectin
¼ tsp. almond extract (optional, but gives a great cherry flavor boost)

Pour juice into large kettle. Add sugar and stir well. Place over high heat and bring to a boil, stirring constantly to avoid scorching. Stir in pectin. Bring to a full rolling boil and boil for 1 minute, stirring constantly.

Remove from heat. Skim if desired. Stir in extract. Pour into previously boiled, hot jars to within ¼ inch of top. Wipe jar rim. Place hot, previously simmered lid on jar and screw down ring firmly tight. Water bath for 5 minutes.

If you are a little short on chokecherries (and it takes a lot to make 3 cups juice in dry years), you can boil the chokecherries in apple juice instead of water and simply use the recipe in powdered pectin for cherry jelly. You can't tell the difference.

Pulp from jelly making

You are such an inspiration to people like me who are just starting out the homesteading lifestyle. I can never wait patiently for your next installment. My question is this: could you, instead of cooking them with a little water until mushy, use an electric juicer to get all of the juice out of berries to make jellies? It's really sad to have so much damp pulp left in the cheesecloth after a jelly-making session, and not be able to squeeze it without turning the jelly cloudy. Would a juicer make the resulting jelly cloudy?

Jessica Andrus, Michigan

Yes! You can use a steam juicer to remove the juice from fresh fruits. And yes, you do get more juice that way. I often cheat if I don't have much of a kind of one fruit. I sometimes run apple juice through the pulp, heating it well again, then using mixed juice, which tastes and looks like, say, chokecherry. And I also have cheated by squeezing the bag. Yep, you do get cloudy jelly, but you know what? Nobody has ever complained! Of course it wouldn't win a prize at the fair, but it sure tastes better than no jelly!

Canned fruit jellies

Would you please tell me if it is possible to make jams and jellies out of fruit I have canned over the years? They are canned using the recipes in the "Ball Blue Book," so there is a bit of sugar in them. The blue and blackberries are whole, the peaches and nectarines are pieces of all sizes, as they were not freestone by any means. If I were to be able to use them, would I use the liquid they are canned in?

Shannan Sweeney, Florida

Yes, you can make jams and preserves out of previously-canned fruits. I've done this with some of mine that had frozen during our move here, making the fruit too soft to be appetizing. Simply drain the syrup from the fruit and continue as with fresh fruit. Jelly won't work because the fruit juice that you normally extract from the fresh fruit has partially seeped out into the syrup and there's no way to measure just how much is water and sugar and juice and sugar.

Sometimes you'll have to kind of experiment around here, but if I can do it, you can do it! Make small batches, one at a time, and adjust as you need to (sugar and/or pectin where desired).

Pomegranate jelly

Can you please tell me how to make pomegranate jelly?

Jacki Clayton

I have never made pomegranate jelly, but I wouldn't be afraid to give it a try.

If you want to give it a shot, I'd suggest using 5 pints of pomegranate seeds, raw. Add to ½ cup water and bring to simmer. Mash seeds gently and simmer for 10 minutes. Line bowl with 3 layers of damp cheesecloth and pour mashed pomegranate seeds and juice. Gather the cheesecloth, making a bag, and hang over the bowl by stout string overnight. In the morning, gently squeeze the bag to get more juice. In large saucepan, add 4 cups juice and 1 envelope of Sure-Jell. Measure 6 cups of sugar into another bowl and set aside till later. Have ready several half-pint jars, as well as lids and rings, that have been sterilized by boiling in water. Bring the juice and pectin to a boil, stirring constantly. Stir in the sugar after the juice comes to a rolling boil that cannot be stirred down. Return to full rolling boil and boil exactly one minute, stirring constantly. Ladle quickly into hot waiting jars to within ⅛ inch of top. Wipe jar rims with damp cloth and place lids on jars. Quickly tighten rings firmly tight. Invert jars for five minutes, then turn upright and place in water bath canner for 10 minutes of processing time (time starts when water bath canner reaches rolling boil). Be sure to have very hot water in water bath canner before the jelly is ladled into jars. Remove from canner and allow jars to stand at room temperature until cooled. Check seals, then wash jars before storing.

I can't guarantee this recipe, but I sure wouldn't be afraid to try it. The worst thing that would happen would be that it wouldn't jell, and you'd end up with pomegranate syrup, which sounds great over homemade vanilla ice cream. And the best that could happen is that it would turn out great the first time and you have a new family heirloom recipe.

However, I do guarantee that the food product would keep and be very edible. I've had to invent recipes for many jams and jellies made from wild fruits, especially since there are few "real" recipes available for them. It's really a lot of fun to experiment a bit with jams and jellies.

Tips on pomegranate jelly

Regarding your reader's question in issue 68 on pomegranate jelly: I've done it for several years and after the first batch didn't jell, I contacted the Certo people, who suggested doubling the pectin to 2 packages instead of one. Also I add 2 Tbsp. fresh lemon juice to the mix.

Incidentally, pomegranates benefit from frost before harvesting. My kids in high school commented when we first harvested and processed them, "You mean there really is something to do with them besides throwing them at other kids?"

Mary Fuller, New Mexico

Thanks, Mary, for your tips on pomegranate jelly. We all appreciate it.

Habañero jelly

My habañero peppers went crazy wild this year. I've been dehydrating them, then grinding to a powder. I have well over a quart and a half of the powder. Probably enough for the next 10 years. They are still coming on strong, so I wondered about trying hot pepper jelly. Can't find it in my Ball book or any other. Do you know of a recipe for habañero jelly? Or perhaps any use for them (besides regular cooking)?

Dani Payne, Oklahoma

Sure Dani, here's one habañero jelly recipe you might like. You already know to use gloves when handling these fire-breathing peppers!

Habañero jelly:

10 ripe habañeros
3 large orange bell peppers
9 oz. liquid pectin
1½ cups white vinegar
7 cups sugar

Remove stems, seeds, and membranes from all peppers. Use gloves. Put peppers and vinegar in a blender and whiz till smooth. Combine pepper purée and sugar in an enameled pan and bring to a boil. Reduce heat and simmer for 20 minutes, stirring frequently to keep from scorching. Remove from heat and strain through cheesecloth into another pan. Add pectin and bring to a full rolling boil while stirring. Boil one minute and ladle into hot sterile jars. Process in a boiling water bath canner for 10 minutes to ensure a seal.

If you like your peppers hot, you might try making cherry jelly with pie cherries or wild cherries and simmering a couple seeded, de-membraned habañeros with the juice and sugar as it's boiling. This makes a real spicy, fruity jelly dip for chicken or fish, and also a good fruity glaze as well. I make this with jalapeños because my crew doesn't like their "hot" that hot!

Jams and preserves

Strawberry jam not setting

A friend and I canned 53 jars of strawberry jam two days ago and it's not set up the way it should. It's a bit runnier than we think it should be. What alternatives do we have to salvage the berry mixture? Neither of us really wants 53 jars of strawberry syrup.

Joan Dove, Washington

Hopefully, all you will need to do is to wait a few weeks. Strawberry jam sometimes takes that long to become as firm as you'd like. But if not, what I would do is to open one jar at a time as you need it, dump it into a saucepan, bring to a boil and add one tablespoon of strawberry gelatin powder. Stir until it is completely dissolved and pour back into the washed, rinsed, still warm jar. (This is one application where you can reuse the lid.)

Set this jar into the fridge when cool, and keep it there after opening. I'm assuming you used pint or half-pint jars. If you used quart jars, use two tablespoons of gelatin. I've done this with good success. You may have to adjust the gelatin a bit, but after the first jar, you'll have it down to a fine science. The jam will be set perfectly and will taste no different.

Causes of runny jam and jelly are: not enough powdered pectin to the batch, too much sugar, not boiling the mixture long enough after adding the sugar, and cooking up a double (or larger batch). Luckily, it's still all edible.

Still, remember to make use of some of those jars of "strawberry syrup." We love strawberry syrup drizzled over homemade vanilla ice cream or an angel food cake.

Jam not setting

I have a situation where I am trying to make strawberry preserves or jam. I have tried both ways. The first time I made jam, I followed the directions explicitly on the box of Ball liquid pectin, and it didn't set up. The second time, I used powdered Sure-Jell, but didn't smash the berries. It didn't set up either. Is there any way to save it? I don't know what I've done wrong.

C. Morris

Did the jam not set right away? This is normal. Many times strawberry jam does not set for a few days. I hope you kept the jam! If it doesn't set, no big loss. You'll love it over pancakes, waffles, or as a dip for your French toast.

It's also great on ice cream, or drizzled over vanilla pudding or frozen yogurt.

If you follow the directions on your pectin product, you will get strawberry jam that sets; it just doesn't always set up right away.

To be sure your jam sets, you can skip the pectin method and use the old-fashioned method, using only strawberries and sugar. It takes more strawberries and sugar, and takes longer to cook, but it will set, right before your eyes. This is how to do it:

Strawberry jam:

2 quarts ripe strawberries
6 cups sugar

Wash strawberries and remove stems. Mash them well with a potato masher. Combine strawberries and sugar in a large kettle. Slowly bring to a boil, stirring until sugar dissolves. Raise heat and boil rapidly, stirring frequently, or it will scorch. As it thickens, stir more often. When it reaches the jelling point, a clean spoonful of the hot jam will slide in a sheet off the side of a spoon, instead of dripping off in drops. When this point is reached, ladle hot jam into hot jars, leaving ¼ inch of headroom. Process 15 minutes in a boiling water bath.

Good luck. In jam making, there are no failures, just a few times the jam doesn't set.

Soupy peach jam

I canned up 12 jars of peach jam last night and they are all soupy. What would cause this?

Victoria

Well, Victoria, it could be the phases of the moon or the will of demons, but probably you simply goofed in your recipe. I do it often enough to be embarrassed. Not too severely, though. I just use it for syrup. Causes? Not measuring correctly, not cooking the jam down enough, not following directions to a T, adding too much water to begin cooking down the jam. Possibly faulty pectin, if you used it. But probably not. Take heart. Your very next batch will probably turn out perfectly because you'll really follow directions this time. It works for me for a few dozen times, then someone calls on the phone or the stock gets out during my jelly and jam making and I screw up again. But one thing's sure — the syrupy jam and jelly sure does taste great.

Redoing jam

I have made jam for years and this year the one batch of strawberry jam is runny. Can I put it back in a pan and bring to a boil with added pectin, and boil again, then put back into jars and reseal?

Name withheld

This is bound to happen sometime during a person's canning experience. I should know; it happens about one batch every year with me. The reason is usually being in too much of a hurry and not following directions to the letter or from doubling a recipe.

I've never felt compelled to remake runny jam or jelly. I simply use it in place of syrup. This is great on pancakes, home-baked rolls and bread, or in flavored yogurt and ice cream. With the ice cream, you can use it as a topping or whip it into the nearly frozen ice cream, then freeze a bit more. It's to die for.

If you really must have a thicker jam product, I wouldn't advise redoing the batch, as you will probably end up with a tough, rubbery jam. Instead, when you open a jar of jam dump it in a saucepan, bring it to a boil, then quickly stir in the same-flavored Jello. Try using a teaspoonful for a pint, two teaspoonfuls for a quart. If this is not firm enough, redo that batch and add more Jello. After it cools in the fridge, it will be nicely jelled. The only hitch is that you have to keep the jam in the fridge and that you have to do this every time you open a new jar of jam.

Unsealed raspberry jam

I canned some raspberry jam three weeks ago and some of the jars didn't seal. Are they good to eat, or should I throw them away?

Rita LaPointe, California

Unless the jars are moldy or smell fermented, they are fine to eat. I would keep them in the fridge until you use them, as they could mold or ferment. But jam will not cause "food poisoning."

To prevent sealing failures in the future, be sure you process the jars of jam in a boiling water bath after screwing down the rings. This eliminates 99% of failed seals in jams and jellies and is why I always do it.

Losing seal on jams during transport

I am a longtime jam maker. I have never had this problem before.

I try taking jam over the Sierra Nevada Mountains from San Jose, California, to Reno, Nevada, and I lose seals on half my jars. It happens when we go over the high mountain passes. Would pressure canning help? But would it ruin my jam? I have never pressure canned before, but would consider it if my jam could travel to my grandson!

Linda Kiel, California

Are you water bath processing your jams or just sealing them when they are hot? If they are water bath processed for 10 minutes (unless a recipe calls for longer), they should not come unsealed. I've hauled my pantry full of home canned foods, including many jams, jellies, and preserves over plenty of very high mountain passes, often four or five at one trip, and never had a bit of trouble with them coming unsealed. My guess is that they are sealed by the older method of pouring boiling jam into hot sterilized jars and then having the lid and ring tightened down. These will seal. But sometimes, not well enough to endure stress. No, I wouldn't advise pressure canning them; jams and jellies often get tough when you do this.

Pear-vanilla jam

Someone mentioned their pear-vanilla bean jam. Wouldn't give the recipe! But, I was positive you would have one. I've made pear jam and was wondering if just adding vanilla bean was the answer. The question is: how much? It sounds really good!

Tess Graves, Georgia

Yep, I do have a recipe and it *is* very good! Here it is:

Pear-vanilla jam:

8 cups chopped pears, peeled
2 vanilla beans, split and scraped
4 cups sugar
1 packet liquid pectin (3 oz.)

In a large pot, combine pears, sugar, and vanilla beans plus the gooey scrapings inside. Cook over medium heat until the fruit is soft. Remove the solid vanilla beans and, using a potato masher, break down the fruit into a smooth sauce.

Add the pectin, bring to a boil, and boil for 5 minutes.

Fill your half-pint sized jars, leaving ¼ inch of headspace. Wipe rims to remove any residual jam. Apply hot, previously simmered lids and screw the rings down firmly tight.

Process the filled jars in a boiling water bath canner for 10 minutes.

Differing jam recipes

My husband and I have recently begun canning for ourselves, and we are really loving it. We are noticing that instructions are different for jams everywhere we look — from how much sugar to add, to what temperature it's ready to be canned at. For example, the Ball canning book is different than the instructions in the Ball pectin. Can you explain this?

Jaime Hogsett, Wisconsin

There is no one recipe for even one kind of jam. Or anything else you may want to cook. There are dozens and dozens of different ones, all of which work fine. Any time I make a food, I choose a recipe (usually one that has worked well for me before, but I do experiment) and follow it.

Some jam recipes use juice for part of the pectin needed to jell the jam. Others use only the pectin in the fruit. Still others use powdered or liquid pectin. Some, you only add sugar and boil and boil to get the jam to jell. Don't let it worry you; they'll all work fine. If you have limited fruit for your jam, you might use a powdered pectin product because you get more end product with your recipe. If you have lots of sugar and time, as well as plenty of fruit, you can choose a recipe without powdered pectin to save money. Again, there is no "right" recipe. Good canning!

Tomatillo jam

I work at a public library and recently had a patron looking for a recipe for tomatillo jam. Believe it or not, I couldn't find one in any of our recipe books. Of course, by that time I was determined to come up with a recipe for this woodsy-looking gentleman. So I thought, who better to ask than Jackie Clay? Do you have anything related to tomatillo jam, jelly, or preserves?

Richda McNutt

One recipe for tomatillo jam calls for 4½ cups husked tomatillos run through a food grinder with a coarse knife. Add 2 cups of sugar, ½ teaspoon ground cinnamon, and ½ teaspoon ground cloves. Bring to a boil, stirring constantly until thickened. It should sheet off a cool teaspoon, not run off in drops. Pour into hot, sterilized jars to within half an inch of the top. Wipe the rim of the jar clean. Place hot, previously boiled lids on the jars and screw the rings down firmly tight. Process in boiling water bath for 10 minutes. Or just pour into jars, cool, then refrigerate. This is very good.

You can also add chopped walnuts for a conserve, instead of a jam.

Tomato jam

Would you please be so kind as to print a recipe for tomato jam? I've seen a few, but I trust your skill with these.

Tess Graves, Georgia

Here's Grandma's recipe for tomato preserves; it's the best recipe I've found for any type of tomato jam/preserves!

Tomato jam:

5 lbs. firm red or yellow tomatoes (Grandma used yellow pear.)
8 lbs. sugar
1 lemon, sliced thin
1 tsp. ground ginger

Skin and cut up tomatoes (dip them in boiling water to slip skins). Add remaining ingredients. Simmer slowly until thick, stirring frequently to prevent scorching. (About 45 minutes.)

Pour into hot sterilized jars, leaving ¼ inch of headspace. Process 10 minutes in a boiling water bath canner. If you live at an altitude above 1,000 feet, consult your canning book for directions on increasing the time to suit your altitude.

If you use yellow tomatoes, you'll have a bright yellow jam; if you use red ones, you'll have a pretty red preserve. Mix 'em and you'll have an orange treat.

Watermelon preserves

I would like to know if you have a recipe for watermelon preserves.

Aniya

Here is one recipe for a type of watermelon preserves, called watermelon balls. You could slice the melon, instead, if you want a less chunky preserve.

Watermelon balls:

10 cups watermelon balls, seedless
¼ cup salt
2 quarts cold water
3 sliced lemons, seeded
4½ cups granulated sugar
2 Tbsp. crystallized ginger

Cut balls from firm pink watermelon with a scoop, picking out the seeds. Soak overnight in mixed salt and water. Drain and rinse in cold water. Add the lemon, sugar, and ginger. Add enough water to cover the fruit. Cook slowly until clear, about 20 minutes. Pick out fruit and place in hot, sterilized jars. Boil the remaining syrup until it threads and pour over fruit and seal. Makes about 3 pints.

Another of our favorite watermelon recipes is sweet watermelon pickles and here's that one, as long as you're doing watermelon.

Double sweet watermelon rind pickles:

3 quarts trimmed watermelon rind
boiling water
10 cups granulated sugar
2 cups vinegar
½ tsp. oil of cloves or 1 tsp. whole cloves
1½ tsp. oil of cinnamon or 1 tsp. ground cinnamon
1 lemon

A thick rind from a garden fresh watermelon is best. Trim off the green skin and any red meat. Cut into one-inch cubes. Place in a large saucepan. Cover with water and simmer about 10 minutes, until tender but not soft. They will appear nearly clear. Drain well. Combine one half of the sugar, all of the vinegar, and seasonings in a saucepan and bring to a boil. Pour over the rinds. Let stand overnight at room temperature. The next day, drain the syrup from the rinds, add the remaining sugar, heat to boiling, and pour over the rinds again. Let stand overnight. On the third and final day, slice the lemon thinly and quarter each slice, then add to the watermelon rind and syrup. Heat to boiling and place in hot, sterilized jars. Wipe the rims of the jars clean, place previously boiled, hot new lids on the jars, and screw down the ring firmly tight. Water bath for 10 minutes. Makes 4-6 pints of "gherkin-sweet" pickle that is pretty and sure to be asked for at holiday meals. (The reason for all the reboiling is that when you make a super sweet pickle, adding too much sugar all at once will shrivel your pickles, making them unappetizing.)

Boiling time for pumpkin preserves

You talked about pumpkin uses. You gave a recipe for pumpkin preserves. It reads fine until you talk about the final procedure. You say to let it stand overnight and in the morning to boil slowly, stirring well. But you don't say anything about how long to boil.

Kathy Vilseck

It will depend on the moisture in the pumpkin you are using. Most just need to be brought up to a simmering boil, then processed. But some are a bit watery, often due to the variety or the amount of rain/irrigation they received. This type needs to be simmered while being stirred until it reaches a nice texture. Then it is processed. Sorry for not explaining myself well enough.

Canning lemon curd

I love lemon curd. Can I can it in jars in the water processor? I hope I can, making it every week or so is getting a bit much!

Jonica Kelly, Maryland

I found this information for you from the University of Georgia and I know I'll use it too:

Canned lemon curd:

2½ cups superfine sugar
½ cup lemon zest (freshly zested) optional
1 cup bottled lemon juice
¾ cup unsalted butter, chilled, cut into approximately ¾-inch pieces
7 large egg yolks
4 large whole eggs

Special equipment needed: lemon zester, balloon whisk, 1½ quart double boiler (the top double boiler pan should be at least 1½-quart volume), strainer, kitchen thermometer measuring at least up to 180°F, glass or stainless steel medium mixing bowl, silicone spatula or cooking spoon, and equipment for boiling water canning. Yield: About 3 to 4 half-pint jars

Procedure:

1. Wash 4 half-pint canning jars with warm, soapy water. Rinse well; keep hot until ready to fill. Prepare canning lids according to manufacturer's directions.

2. Fill boiling water canner with enough water to cover the filled jars by 1 to 2 inches. Use a thermom-

eter to preheat the water to 180°F by the time filled jars are ready to be added. Caution: Do not heat the water in the canner to more than 180°F before jars are added. If the water in the canner is too hot when jars are added, the process time will not be long enough. The time it takes for the canner to reach boiling after the jars are added is expected to be 25 to 30 minutes for this product. Process time starts after the water in the canner comes to a full boil over the tops of the jars.

3. Combine the sugar and lemon zest in a small bowl, stir to mix, and set aside about 30 minutes. Premeasure the lemon juice and prepare the chilled butter pieces.

4. Heat water in the bottom pan of the double boiler until it boils gently. The water should not boil vigorously or touch the bottom of the top double boiler pan or bowl in which the curd is to be cooked. Steam produced will be sufficient for the cooking process to occur.

5. In the top of the double boiler, on the countertop or table, whisk the egg yolks and whole eggs together until thoroughly mixed. Slowly whisk in the sugar and zest, blending until well mixed and smooth. Blend in the lemon juice and then add the butter pieces to the mixture.

6. Place the top of the double boiler over boiling water in the bottom pan. Stir gently but continuously with a silicone spatula or cooking spoon to prevent the mixture from sticking to the bottom of the pan. Continue cooking until the mixture reaches a temperature of 170°F. Use a food thermometer to monitor the temperature.

7. Remove the double boiler pan from the stove and place on a protected surface, such as a dish cloth or towel on the countertop. Continue to stir gently until the curd thickens (about 5 minutes). Strain curd through a mesh strainer into a glass or stainless steel bowl; discard collected zest.

8. Fill hot strained curd into the clean, hot half-pint jars, leaving ½-inch headspace. Remove air bubbles and adjust headspace if needed. Wipe rims of jars with a dampened, clean paper towel; apply two-piece metal canning lids.

9. Process half pints in the prepared boiling water canner 15 minutes for 0-1,000 feet altitude, 20 minutes for 1,001 to 6,000 feet altitude, and 25 minutes above 6,000 feet altitude. Let cool, undisturbed, for 12 to 24 hours and check for seals.

Fruits

Artificial sweeteners for canning

Please ask Jackie if you can use Sweet'n Low or any artificial sweetener for canning instead of regular sugar. Both my husband and I are hypoglycemics and cannot have sugar. I know commercial canners do. What about home canning (jellies, jams, tomatoes etc.)?

Ron & Bernice Knapp, Kansas

Canning without sugar is no problem. My husband, Bob, is diabetic so we have to watch sugar pretty closely. With all fruit, simply can without it. Then, as it is opened, sprinkle your sugar substitute over the fruit. It's much better this way than when canned with the sugar substitute. Sugar does nothing but flavor the fruit.

When putting up jams and jellies, I use sugar-free Sure-Jell. You can use artificial sweeteners in your jams and jellies as well, but you must use a recipe that does not call for sugar, as some recipes need the sugar to make the jelly jell. One note: If you use aspartame, add it toward the end of your jam or jelly's boiling, as boiling drastically reduces the sweetness of this artificial sweetener.

Another option is to use very ripe fruits (but not to the spoiling point) without any sweetener, simply boiling gently to concentrate the juice, then canning as "fruit." On opening, either use as a spread, sprinkled with artificial sweetener if desired, or mix the canned fruit spread with enough sugar-free Jello to jell. You'll have to experiment a bit, as this depends on your fruit and how thick you'll want it. This product may be placed back into the canning jar, but must be refrigerated or it will spoil.

For other canning recipes calling for sugar, you can often substitute such things as very sweet, ripe tomatoes or reconstituted dried tomatoes (which are much sweeter), using more herbs and/or adding artificial sweeteners.

Most newer canning books include a section on sugar-free canning. You can also check with your county extension office for free or low-cost leaflets on sugar-free canning.

It's best to use one of these guides, at least until you get the hang of it. One thing you'll quickly discover is that home canned sugar-free foods are worlds above the store-bought foods, and a whole lot cheaper to boot.

Sugar-free canning

I would like to know where I can find recipes for sugar-free canning. I love to can but hate all that sugar. I presently can jam using only honey, but I need some varied recipes with no sugar.

Name withheld

Any fruits can be canned sugar-free, using only fruit juice and the fruits' natural sweetness. Sugar does nothing regarding canning keepability. As for sugar-free jam and jelly recipes, check out a box of any sugar-free pectin product at your supermarket. There are a lot of recipes listed, and best yet, they're pretty good, too.

Elderberry concentrate

When elderberry concentrate approached $35 for two cups, I started making it from my own elderberry bushes. My neighbor and I would like to know if you have a method for making elderberry concentrate.

Here is how I do it, but I have no clue if it is correct. The strength and taste seem to vary:

1. Berries are washed, removed from the stem, and washed again.

2. With only the clean water clinging to them after draining, they are put in a pressure cooker.

3. The pressure is built up until the indicator rises. It stays risen for 30 seconds to one minute, and then I switch off the heat.

4. After the berries cool, they are put in a "jelly bag" (a fine mesh nylon curtain from the thrift shop), and drain overnight into a large, shallow, ceramic cookware pan.

5. The next day, I evaporate the juice in the pan by one-third, sometimes more. I do not know if this is necessary. The juice is no thicker at the finish than at the start. It would be like "evaporating" water and expecting it to "thicken." This step could be a time waster.

6. I have learned NOT to squeeze the bag to get out the last bit of juice. Otherwise, there is a green, sticky residue that destroys the bag for future use and coats pan, sink, and utensils. Worse than Gorilla Glue to try to budge, even with hot water and soap and scrubber. Do you know what this green sticky stuff is?

7. While the "evaporated" juice is still hot, I stir in honey to taste, let it all cool, bottle in 1-quart plastic milk bottles, and put in the freezer.

8. Is it safe to use the plastic milk bottles more than once (or at all) or will the bad stuff in the plastic start to leach out?

I can use the elderberry juice just as it is used for the commercial products; 1 to 2 Tbsp. in a cup of hot water as a nightcap. It doesn't taste as rich as the commercial, and it isn't as syrupy, but it is still pretty darn good.

Sharon Cregier, Prince Edward Island

Obviously, your method works. Sure I know what that green glue is: it's green sticky stuff. Seriously, I really don't know, but I do know what you mean from my jelly-making experiences.

The way I make elderberry concentrate is quicker than your method. Not necessarily better. I just simmer the elderberries in a large kettle with very little water and the top on, stirring to mash them as they cook. Then I jelly bag them overnight and freeze the juice in wide-mouth jars or even plastic jugs, filling them only two-thirds full. In the morning, I set the jars on the counter to thaw, watching carefully. The first to thaw is the concentrated juice. The last to thaw is mostly water. Just pour off the first-to-melt juice and leave the ice "cone" in the jug. Mix this with honey or corn syrup (a lot of commercial products use corn syrup for that "rich, syrupy" taste) and you are in business. You can home can this product or freeze it as you wish.

Yes, you can use the plastic milk bottles more than once, but I really hate plastic and prefer glass jars myself.

Processing elderberries

I am trying to find info on how to process elderberries. I have a press that I can use to get the extract, but do you heat the berries before you press? If so, what temperature and how long? How long do you pressure can them to save the extract?

Wayne Creasser, Kansas

Check out the previous question as it will answer some of your questions. To home can the juice, heat it to boiling, pour it into hot, sterilized jars, and process it in a boiling water bath canner for 15 minutes. That's all there is to it. Good luck!

Blackberries

I have 60 lbs. of blackberries and if it doesn't frost I might get more than 100 lbs. of them. Other than jam, what is the best way to keep them?

Rich

Wow, Rich, you've hit a gold mine. Oh my, what can you do with all of them? Well you could freeze them to use as fresh. I don't generally like to freeze things, but berries freeze so well and taste amazingly like fresh; it's a good way to go. Simply spread them out on a cookie sheet and drop them in the freezer. Just as soon as they're frozen, bag them up, making sure most of the air is out of the bag. You can sprinkle them with sugar as you bag them, if you'd like. They won't keep but about six months, but I doubt if you will have them that long.

Or you can dehydrate them. This is easy, too. Just spread them out in a single layer on a dehydrator tray or cookie sheet. Dehydrate at about 150°F until they are like tough raisins. If you use the cookie sheet, you can use your gas oven with only the pilot light on. It's best to scrape them around about halfway through, so the entire berry dries. You can even use the backseat of your car on a warm sunny day to dry the berries.

These are great in muffins or pancakes. Just toss a handful in the batter and bake. Or for a pie, simply soak for about an hour in warm water, drain, and use as fresh.

Blackberries can up quite nicely, too. Simply fix a syrup mixture of water and as much or little sugar as you prefer and boil that. Then add the berries to a jar, gently thumping the jar down to settle the berries snugly without mashing them, to within half an inch of the top of the jar. Then fill the jar to within half an inch of the top with the hot, boiled syrup. Process the jars 15 minutes for pints and 20 minutes for quarts in a boiling water bath.

Or you can make blackberry pancake and ice cream syrup from the blackberries. In a large kettle pour enough water to cover the bottom an inch or so deep. Add the berries and begin to heat, mashing the berries with a potato masher. Stir well as you juice the berries. Strain off juice, either overnight with a jelly bag, or through a strainer, removing the seeds and pulp. Then add four cups of juice to one cup of sugar and cook until as thick as you want. Pour into hot pint jars and process 15 minutes in a boiling water bath. This is excellent and also makes a tasty treat when you've got a sore throat.

Canning pears

About 10 years ago a friend told me about how she canned her pears without peeling them. What you do is wash, halve, and core the fruit, but leave the skins on the pears, and place in your canning jars. Add your syrup, make to your preference, and process. This method will save hours of the very boring chore of paring, and you process twice as many pears in less time. If you really object to the skin on the pears, it will slip off when you open the jars to serve the fruit. Once you try canning pears with this method, you will never go back to peeling, and the extra benefit is the flavor is much better.

C. Ronna Jordan, New York

I've canned crabapples this way, only removing the cores and stems. The skins were thin enough that I could make apple pie from them and you didn't even notice the skins. Peeling is just a personal thing, sort of like eating potato peels; some folks love 'em and others wouldn't be caught dead with an intact potato on their plates.

Discolored canned fruit

Last year I canned up a bunch of pears that I got for free from a woman who didn't have the time.

The first batch I canned cold packed in pint jars; the rest I hot packed after realizing how much they shrink during heating, again in pint jars. Most of them look wonderful, but the jars from the first batch that I cold packed are discolored on top. The seals are intact, but the contents are browned on top. The rest (hot packed) did not do this.

What did I do wrong?

Lee Robertson, Michigan

You didn't do anything wrong. When you cold pack many food items, the fruit tends to float to the top. When you leave the needed headspace or air space at the top of the jar, this air can darken some foods, such as your pears, or shrivel the pickles that are out of the brine. This food is unappetizing to look at, but is not "bad." I simply take a fork and remove the ugly food and go on and use the rest. For pretty food that packs better in the jars, hot pack the food. I'll admit that when I'm in a hurry, I just jam the cold food into the jar and get it into the canner. If I get a few bits of ugly food, I just remove it before serving it.

Foolproof recipe for canning pears

My wife and I have recently made the decision to pursue a more self-reliant form of daily living, as we both are subscribers to BHM. *Do you have or know where we could obtain an absolutely foolproof recipe for canning soups and pears (or similar fruit)? We basically are looking for pressures and boiling times. As you know, there are so many recipes out there that we have gotten quite confused reading these.*

Troy and Michelle Hammond, Michigan

As for fruits, pears are about as easy as any, but nearly all of them are processed the same way. First, a sugar syrup is boiled to dissolve the sugar entirely. This syrup can be made as thin or as syrupy thick as you want; it does little to make the fruit "keep." My husband is diabetic, so I can much of our fruit in a very light syrup, which is rinsed off on serving. Other families have a sweet tooth and make really sweet canned fruit. Make your syrup as follows:

For thin syrup, mix 1 cup of sugar with 3 cups of water; medium syrup is 1 cup of sugar with 2 cups of water; and heavy syrup is 1 cup of sugar in 1 cup of water. You may double or triple the recipe if you have a kettle large enough to let this come to a complete boil (and not boil over on your stove — what a mess).

For any fruit, peel and cut up into the size you desire. I cold pack nearly all my fruit just because I can get it done quicker. In cold packing, the first step is to peel, then pack the fruit into clean canning jars. The only problem is that cold packed fruit tends to float to the top of the syrup somewhat. But there's no difference in taste or keeping qualities. With hot packed fruit the first step is to peel, then dump the fruit into your hot syrup, which is then heated to boiling and dipped out into jars.

Whichever method you use, the rest of the process is to fill the jars with fruit to within ½ inch of the top, and pour hot syrup in to within ½ inch of the top, as well.

Then wipe the rim of the jar, place a hot, previously boiled lid in place, and screw down the ring firmly tight. Pints of pears are processed for 20 minutes in a boiling water bath, which covers the jars by at least 1 inch. Be absolutely sure that the jars rest on a rack above the kettle bottom. If they do not, they will usually crack.

As with all canning, get a good canning book, such as the *Ball Blue Book: The Guide to Home Canning and Freezing*, available at many stores or Lehman's, 888-438-5346. I refer to my canning books every time I can, just to be sure. (And I've never poisoned anyone yet, unlike a few fast food joints I know of.)

Canning grapefruit

I was wondering if you have ever heard of canning fresh picked grapefruit. I have a new home in southwest Florida and I have Ruby Red grapefruits and would love to can them. Can you help with this?

Chris Vest, Florida

Yes. Actually, grapefruit sections are very easy to can. The hardest part is sectioning the grapefruits.

First, section each grapefruit, removing any seeds. Prepare a thin syrup (4 cups water or juice mixed with 2 cups of sugar or honey). Fill hot jars with sections, leaving ½ inch of headroom. Add boiling thin syrup, leaving ½ inch of headroom. Cap. Process in a boiling water bath for 10 minutes for either pints or quarts.

(With grapefruit being very juicy, it is usually best to use the "left over" grapefruit juice to make your syrup, as the taste of the finished product is better.) It's great you have your own. Lucky you!

Canning persimmons

How do I can persimmons? I know they freeze well, but I want a longer shelf life, maintaining their color. Have you ever used a steam canner and can you give me information on using one?

Elaine Berry, California

Persimmons are really better dried, looking like slices of dried fig, or eaten fresh. But you can home can them, if you'd like.

> Simply mash the very ripe persimmons and run them through a sieve, if you have a variety with seeds. Fill half-pint or pint jars with the pulp to within half an inch of the rim. Wipe the rim clean and put a hot, previously boiled lid on the jar. Screw down the ring firmly tight and process for 30 minutes in a hot water bath canner.

A steam canner is not a safe way to can, as there is a possibility of the temperature not being even throughout the canner, jars, and food. A water bath canner is the safest way to process high-acid foods. And it's cheaper, too.

Canning lemon juice

I have canned over half of my life and I would like to tell you the recipes I have tried from your column are fantastic. I would like to know if there is a way you could can egg drop soup. I also would like to know if you could can your own fresh lemon juice. I get an overabundance of fresh lemons and would like to can the juice for the winter months.

Vicki Thomason, Montana

I'm glad you like my recipes; they're ones we love and use all the time. I know no way of canning egg drop soup, but you can certainly can all the lemon juice you have available. Here's how:

> Cut your lemons in half and juice. Strain to remove seeds. Heat juice 5 minutes to just simmering (190°F). Don't boil. Ladle hot juice into hot jars, leaving ¼ inch of headspace. Seal and process in a boiling water bath canner for 15 minutes.

Don't forget to harvest the lemon zest or grate the peel to dehydrate. Wash the lemons before you juice them, then use a potato peeler or the fine side of your grater to harvest the peel. Don't use the white as it is bitter. Dehydrate the peel. I usually then give the dried peel a spin in my old blender to reduce it to powder. I use it a lot in various recipes, including stir-fries and baking. It is very good!

Canning fruit juices

We want to can fruit juices. Could you please give us a procedure for this? Is pasteurization or sterilization necessary?

Dr. L. A. Ukwuoma

Fruit juice is very easy to home can and it is very rewarding, as it tastes so much better than store bought juices, which are usually diluted and made from less than wonderful fresh fruit. And you know there are no chemicals included in your beverage.

As fruit juice is high acid, it is able to be water bath canned. As high temperatures tend to spoil the pure taste of fresh fruit juice, try to keep your juices from a hard boil, using a simmer instead to extract the juice and also to can it. The process varies from fruit to fruit, and you can check a recent canning manual for exact directions. Here are a few common ones.

Apple juice:

To make apple juice, first you must extract the juice from apples. This is easily done with an apple grinder, which is also used commonly when making cider. The apples are ground to a pulp, then pressed with weight to extract the juice out of a bag of apple pulp. This weight is usually a screw-down type follower that presses down on the pulp held in a slatted wooden cylinder. Most people in apple country are at least familiar with pictures of them.

Once the juice has been pressed, you may want to strain it for clarity. Then pour the juice into sterilized jars, leaving ¼ inch of headspace. Process in a 185°F hot water bath for 30 minutes.

For berry and currant juice:

Extract juice and add sugar, if desired, to taste. Heat to simmer and pour into hot, sterilized jars, leaving ½ inch of headspace. Process in a 190°F hot water bath for 30 minutes.

Grape juice:

Extract juice. Add sugar if desired and bring to a simmer. Pour hot juice into hot sterilized jars, leaving ¼ inch of headspace. Process in a 190°F hot water bath for 30 minutes.

Cherry juice:

Sour cherries make the best juice. If using sweet cherries, add some sour cherries for better flavor. Add sugar to taste. Heat juice and pour into sterilized jars and process in a 185°F hot water bath for 30 minutes.

I hope this will cover the juices you plan on canning.

Storing citrus

I recently moved here to southern Texas where citrus abounds. Can you advise different ways I can store or freeze the oranges and grapefruit I have in my backyard? I hate to just let it go to waste.

Barry Eppley, Texas

You can freeze the juice or home can the sections of fruit or juice. Canning citrus is easy. For instance, to can oranges:

Remove fruit segments, peeling away the white membrane that could cause a bitter taste during the canning. Remove the seeds. Make a light or medium syrup, as you wish, and keep it hot. Pack orange segments in hot jars, gently shaking the jar to settle the fruit, leaving ½ inch of headspace. Ladle boiling syrup over fruit, leaving ½ inch of headspace. Remove air bubbles. Wipe the rim of the jar clean, place hot, previously-simmered lid on jar, and screw down ring firmly tight. Process pints and quarts for 10 minutes in a boiling water bath canner.

To can grapefruit:

Make a light or medium syrup, as you wish. Peel grapefruit with a sharp knife, removing the white membrane. Run your sharp knife between the pulp and skin of each section and lift out the sections without breaking. Remove and discard the seeds. Pack grapefruit in hot jars, leaving ½ inch of headspace. Cover with boiling syrup, leaving ½ inch of headspace. Remove air bubbles. Wipe rim of jar clean, place hot, previously-simmered lid on jar, and screw down ring firmly tight. Process both pints and quarts for 10 minutes in a boiling water bath canner. Enjoy your citrus!

What to do with quinces

I have a lot of old plantings of fruit trees and berries. I have two very prolific quince trees. The fruit is plentiful and relatively pest-free. What should I do with them?

Terry J. Ziellinski

Sounds like you've got a great place, Terry. So few places today come with mature fruit and nut trees. Quinces are one of my childhood favorites. My grandmother had a quince tree growing in our yard, and I loved to watch them grow and turn golden. And I couldn't wait until my grandma said I could climb the tree, picking them to make into preserves. I liked to munch as I picked, even though they were juicy-tart.

You can make jelly, similar to apple jelly, but the following recipes are more to my liking.

Ginger quince jam:

4 lbs. quinces
8 cups sugar
¼ lb. crystallized ginger root
2 lemons

Wash, pare, and core quinces. Chop in fine pieces, cook in moderate amount of boiling water until tender. Add sugar, chopped ginger, and the juice and grated rind of the lemons. Cook until thick, stirring constantly. Pour into sterilized canning jars to within ½ inch of the top. Wipe the rims, put on hot, previously boiled lids, and screw the rings down firmly. Process in boiling water bath for 10 minutes. Yield: 6 half-pints.

Quince apple preserves:

Pare and slice apples and quinces; use half as many apples as you have quinces. For each pound of combined fruits use ¾ pound of sugar. Cook the quinces in boiling water until tender, then add the sugar and apples and cook until apples are tender, while stirring constantly. When thickened, pour into jars, and process as above.

Quince preserves:

3 cups sugar
2 quarts water
7 cups pared, cored, quartered quinces

When preparing quinces, discard all gritty parts. Combine sugar and water in large kettle. Simmer 5 minutes. Add the quinces and cook until they're transparent and the syrup is almost jellying, about 1 hour. Stir regularly to prevent scorching. Pour hot into hot, sterilized jars, leaving ½ inch of headspace. Process as above.

Mincemeat recipes

My grandfather speaks fondly of the mincemeat his mother used to make — "much better than the stuff they sell in the store now." He remembered it the most in sandwiches, not the typical pie. I would like to mince meat for him, but after looking at several recipes, I have several questions.

Did mincemeat originally have (or is it necessary to have) alcohol in it in some form? Some recipes call for brandy, and others cider, and some use a combination. My grandfather didn't remember his mother keeping brandy on hand, but then, he never really watched her make mincemeat, either. At first I was just going to use cider, but almost all cider you can buy has been pasteurized. Wouldn't that affect the taste? And if she never canned it, wouldn't the unpasteurized eventually have some alcohol? Or is it possible that she used vinegar instead? I did find one recipe that called for cider and cider vinegar, and then it was "seasoned to taste" with brandy right before serving. I find it odd to think of alcohol in a child's sandwich, but maybe no one did back then. Any suggestions?

Also, what would be the best way of storing it? The meat is cooked ahead of time. I know a lot of people used to (and maybe still do) just leave it in the crock, or else seal it with "greased paper and twine" or paraffin. Some recipes told me to can it for 20 minutes at 15 pounds for pints (I was going to do half-pints). And I know I've read you're supposed to can meat for 70 minutes, but isn't that for raw meat, not precooked? Would it be better for the taste and texture if I just froze it instead? A lot of the recipes call for citron, but if that used to be easy to find, it sure isn't now. Do you think they usually used fresh citron or candied citron? Is there any chance you could help clear things up for me, or should I just experiment?

Talitha Purdy

I can understand your confusion, as there are so many recipes for "mincemeat." Most of the old recipes for mincemeat did call for brandy. This was both for flavoring and for the preserving qualities. With the sugars and other preservatives, the mincemeat was packed in a crock and kept in a cold place all winter. Today, I would recommend freezing the resultant mincemeat, if it is a mincemeat with minced meat in it. The brandy was put in at the end of the cooking down time and the boiling cooked off most of the alcohol, so the children weren't being fed alcohol.

The citron was candied citron. Folks often grew citron melon and candied the peel as you do watermelon rind pickle to use in different recipes. Store bought candied citron will be fine. Some of my recipes use cider or cider and vinegar. I don't think the pasteurized cider would make a difference, especially if you freeze the mincemeat. (Many women used the brandy, but didn't advertise it.)

Here are two good Amish recipes for mincemeat, one which is a great way to have nonmeat mincemeat from green summer tomatoes.

Abigail Troyer's mincemeat:

1 lb. lean beef, cubed
⅔ cup water
6 cups chopped apples
1 cup raisins
2 cups currants
½ cup chopped orange peel
2 Tbsp. grated lemon peel
¼ cup orange juice
2 Tbsp. lemon juice
2 cups sugar
1 tsp. cinnamon
½ tsp. ground cloves
½ tsp. ground nutmeg
½ tsp. mace
1 tsp. salt
2 cups apple cider
1 cup brandy

In a saucepan bring the water to a boil and cook beef cubes covered for an hour. When the meat has cooled, put it through a food chopper. Combine all the ingredients, except the brandy, in a large saucepan and cook uncovered for two hours, stirring occasionally. When the mixture begins to thicken, add the brandy and cook five minutes longer. Seal in hot, sterilized jars.

Summertime mincemeat:

3 cups chopped green tomatoes
3 cups chopped apples
1 cup vinegar
1 cup molasses
3 cups brown sugar
½ cup butter
1 Tbsp. salt
2 cups raisins
1 tsp. cinnamon
½ tsp. ground cloves
½ tsp. ground ginger

Combine all the ingredients in large kettle. Boil five minutes and seal in hot sterilized jars for pie filling.

Personally, I would recommend either freezing the mincemeats or processing the tomato version in a hot water bath canner for 15 minutes, but these are the original recipes.

Home canning apple pie filling

I was wondering if it is possible to home can apple pie filling, and not just plain apples.

I have instructions for freezing it, but not for canning, and I have four canning books.

Lee Robertson, Michigan

Yes, you may home can apple pie filling. Here's one recipe; you can adjust the spices to suit your taste.

12 lbs. firm apples
4 cups sugar
½ cup flour
3 tsp. cinnamon
½ tsp. nutmeg
4 Tbsp. lemon juice

Peel and slice the apples. Stir in sugar, flour, and spices. When juice is making the mixture wet, stir in lemon juice and cook over a medium heat until it thickens, stirring frequently. Ladle pie filling into hot quart jars to within ½ inch of the top. Wipe the rim clean. Place hot, previously simmered lid on jar and screw down ring firmly tight. Process in water bath canner for 30 minutes.

Experts today do not recommend canning this as it does contain some flour, making it remotely possible to support *Botulinum* bacteria which causes toxins. I have used this recipe in the past and it turned out fine. But I must add this caution or have the experts eat me alive.

Canning pie filling

I just made a batch of strawberry jam and wanted to try and can strawberry-rhubarb pie filling. I am confused as there are only a few recipes out there and some say use cornstarch to thicken and others say you need to use Sure-Jell. Do you know the proper way to can this type of pie filling?

Laurie Goldstein, New York

Use Clear Jel, not Sure-Jell. Clear Jel is a refined cornstarch. The experts tell us that regular cornstarch is not safe enough to use in canning and that we must now use Clear Jel instead. Just replace the amount of cornstarch with Clear Jel in your recipe and you'll be fine. You can usually find Clear Jel online or in stores carrying canning supplies.

Pickles

Canning pickles

I am planning on canning pickles this year, my first canning endeavor. I appreciate your help with these questions. Do I have to use special canning cukes? I'm currently growing a Japanese variety. Can I cut my cukes into quarters? With "raw pack" should the water be at a rolling boil before lowering jars in?

Can I use honey instead of sugar? If so, do you have a conversion table? Can I have only 2 or 3 jars in the pot or does it have to be full?

Jen French

Good luck with your pickling. It's so easy and a lot of fun, actually. To answer your questions: No, you don't need special pickling cukes. I've even used zucchini. I would stay with the way the recipe calls for, such as sliced thinly, cut into chunks, or cut into spears. I'm assuming you want to quarter your Japanese cukes because they're so long they won't fit into the jars right. In this case, you can quarter them, if making spears. It doesn't matter if the end is cut. Have the water at just below a rolling boil, simmering, when you put your jars in, or the steam may burn you. Until you have some pickling experience, I'd recommend that you stick with sugar. Then you can try recipes, switching honey for the sugar. Yes, you can put any number of jars in the hot water bath, even one. Again, great pickling.

Canning with artificial sweetener

I love the site, but couldn't find anything about canning with artificial sweetener. After by-pass surgery in November, I am insulin dependent. I love to can and love pickles. Have you ever heard if it is okay to use sweetener? Thanks so much.

Vonnie

You can use artificial sweetener in many canning recipes. Most canning books, such as the *Blue Ball Book*, often available at your local Wal-Mart, list sugar-free canning recipes. They are also available in many recent canning books. Check out your local library, including inter-library loan.

As my husband, Bob, is a diabetic, we have switched from his "favorite" Bread and Butter pickles to more dills, which have no sugar. I cheat and add artificial sweetener to an opened jar of mild dills then put them in the fridge. After a couple of days they are quite sweet, taking the edge off his sweet tooth.

Here is a recipe for using artificial sweetener. (Don't add NutraSweet, as when it boils it loses "sweet.")

Sweet cuke slices:

10 pounds medium cukes
1 cup salt
2¼ quarts white vinegar
2 Tbsp. Sucaryl solution
½ cup mixed pickle spices

Wash and slice cukes ¼ inch thick. Mix cukes with salt and enough ice water to barely cover. Let sit overnight, covered. In morning, drain and rinse with cold water. Combine vinegar, liquid Sucaryl, and spices. Boil 1 minute. Add cukes and bring to full boil. Immediately pack cukes into clean, hot, sterile jars to within 1 inch of top. Fill jars with hot, spiced vinegar to within ½ inch of top. Wipe rim and seal. Makes about 12 pints.

Mushy pickles

When I can vegetables, meat, or stew, I follow the directions to the letter. Everything except jams and jelly turns out mushy and cloudy, like it's on its way to becoming baby food. I have a friend in medical practice and he tested it for botulism and other bacteria, and it's fine. What am I doing wrong?

When I make pickles, they always go mushy too.

Is it possible to make pickles with something like Everclear, vodka or gin? I'd like to try it and show off to my friends on Super Bowl Sunday. (They're always bringing weird things.)

Dennis C. Nelson, Minnesota

Well Dennis, I see you keep busy, too. But I'll bet you're tired of cloudy, mushy canned food, huh? My best guess is that you have water with a lot of minerals in it. This causes cloudy canned foods and soft, cloudy pickles. If you have naturally soft water available (neighbor or friend), I'd recommend hauling a few five-gallon jugs home at canning time, in which to can your fruits and vegetables.

I'd also have your pressure gauge on your canner checked to ensure it's reading the pressure properly, as an additional problem may be that you may accidently be canning at too high a pressure. Processing for too long a time or using too high a pressure will result in mushy canned foods.

Another thought: you say "go mushy." Is this after storage? Could the jars be freezing during the winter? I had to keep a wood stove going in my Minnesota basement to keep my canning and root cellar crops from freezing during the worst of the winter. Frozen canned goods are good to eat after freezing, if the seals are still good; tight and indented. But the quality of the food is definitely much worse — cloudy and mushy. I learned this when much of my canned goods froze in the U-Haul truck during our "trying to move to British Columbia" fiasco. I'm still trying to use up the canned goods that froze, but some of the green beans, carrots, potatoes, and fruit is not the best. I use it up bit by bit, in mixed dishes, and the fruit in baked desserts.

A tip, besides heavily mineralized water for mushy pickles: don't over-boil your pickles or they'll get soft. When the recipe says "bring to a boil and boil one minute," do just that. Three minutes will make soft, unappetizing pickles.

Sorry, I can't find a recipe for pickles made with alcohol. Anybody out there who can help Dennis?

Pickles

I have been canning for about 5 years. I started out with the simple stuff (jams and jellies) but can quite a variety now. I have been fairly successful, except for my pickled foods. I have attempted pickles (dill, sweet, and sweet and sour) and pickled peppers. They all turn out mushy! I use the "Ball Blue Book" recipe for my pickled peppers and used Mrs. Wages for my pickles this year. I do not use the brine/ferment method. Do you have any suggestions?

Also, while we are discussing peppers, I saw in your last article that you mentioned that green peppers should be pressure canned. Does this include all peppers or just bell peppers? I use red bell peppers in a zucchini relish and the recipe (from "Ball Blue Book") does not say it should be pressure canned. I also use green peppers in my salsa; should I be pressure canning my salsa?

I try to be VERY careful with my home canning, especially since we just spent 3 weeks in the hospital with my 3 year old daughter (she had hemolytic-uremic syndrome [HUS], which is usually caused by E. Coli) and I certainly do not want to go through something like that again!

Marni J. Nelson-Snyder

Do you have a water softener? This is one cause of soft pickles. So is excessive minerals in the water. I've known women who hauled water from a neighbor's spring during pickling season because their own water had too many minerals to make good pickles. I used to make pickles that were too soft, too. Then I talked to a master pickle maker from California, who had won first prize after first prize for his pickles. The secret? Don't boil your pickles too long. That seems simple; the longer you boil vegetables, the softer they become. The same works for pickles, too. It took me years to learn this, but now I am very careful. When the recipe says, "bring the pickles to a boil," it means just that. Don't boil them for 10 minutes or they will be soft. Now my pickles are very firm and crunchy, with no added alum or chemicals. We seldom have leftovers to go back into the fridge.

Like you, I am very careful with my home canning, and can honestly say no one in my family has ever suffered any sort of problem from eating this food. (Except stuffed feelings from eating too much.) On the other hand, we have had food poisoning three times from restaurant food. Gee, let's see … you pay too much for not-so-great food … that makes you sicker than a dog for two or three days. Boy, *that* makes sense, doesn't it?

Keeping homemade pickles crispy

Is there any way to keep your homemade pickles crispy? My mother makes mustard pickles but they sometimes don't stay crispy like the ones in the store.

Sherry Sigler

The best way to keep pickles crisp is not to boil them too long before you water bath them. A very old-time pickle maker told me this secret, and since I really watch my timing, my pickles are always nice and crisp. No, I do not add alum or lime to my pickles to make them crisp. They are just naturally crisp by themselves.

Another thing that will help you make crisp pickles is to pick your produce in the cool morning and immediately wash and process your pickles. And when it says to soak the cukes or beans in ice water, it means just that. Keep those veggies cold and crisp as long as possible. But don't over-chill them, either, by putting them in the freezer for a while or pouring ice over them. These things will result in limp pickles too.

Grape leaves for pickles

I'm fixin' to make crock pickles from your recipe. I remember my dad saying the way to keep pickles crisp was to place a wild grape leaf in each jar. Have you heard of this and if so will this work with your crock recipe?

Bonnie, Missouri

Grape leaves have been used for generations to help keep pickles crisp. Yes, you can certainly use a grape leaf or two in my pickle recipes. My best secret is to not cook the pickles too long during heating and processing. Don't leave them boiling one minute longer than necessary.

Canning dill pickles

My husband asked me to inquire about the possibility of canning dill pickles that would taste similar to those we purchase at our local grocery market. I have refused to attempt this as of yet because I recall several failed attempts by my mother. The dill pickles she produced can only be described as "nasty," even though her sweet pickles were very tasty. Is there a fail-safe procedure or recipe you can recommend to us?

Mrs. Sean Evans, Oregon

Most failures in dill pickles result from the long method, where dill pickles are brined in a large crock. While this can result in very good pickles, sometimes one forgets to skim the scum that forms on top of the brine every day or doesn't get the top plate, which holds the pickles under the brine weighted down enough to keep the pickles covered with brine. The result is mushy, nasty pickles. Try this quick dill method which is the one I most often use. (I've no time for scum skimming.) I think you and your husband will enjoy them.

Fresh-pack dill pickles:

18 lbs. of 3 to 5 inch cukes
1½ cups plus ¾ cup salt
2 gallons plus 9 cups water
6 cups vinegar
¼ cup sugar
21 heads of dill *or* 1 cup dill seed
2 Tbsp. pickling spice
⅓ cup mustard seed
7 cloves garlic
7 small, dry hot pepper pods

Thoroughly wash, rinse, and drain the cucumbers. Cover them with a brine made of 1½ cups salt and 2 gallons cold water and let stand overnight. Rinse and drain the cukes. Mix the vinegar, 9 cups of water, the remaining ¾ cup salt, sugar, mixed spices (tied in a cloth bag), and heat to a boil. Keep hot. Pack cucumbers to within half an inch of the top of quart jars. Put 2 teaspoons mustard seed, 1 clove peeled garlic, 3 heads of dill (or 1 tablespoon dill seed) and 1 pod of pepper in each jar. Cover cucumbers with hot pickling liquid. Wipe rim. Put on hot, previously boiled lid and screw down ring firmly tight. Process 20 minutes in boiling water bath. Makes 7 quarts.

You can adjust this recipe a little — you may omit garlic or increase it a little, omit the hot pepper or increase — according to your family's taste. Try a batch and make notes to yourself for next time. These pickles work well every time. Use pickling salt, not iodized salt, and be sure you use fresh cukes, not ones that stood around after harvest.

Soft dill pickles

I remember when my aunt made Polish dills. They were so good that I wanted to make kosher dills. I went to the store and bought the "Ball Blue Book" and used their recipe; the pickles came out very soft not crunchy. They went into the trash. What made them soft like that and do you have a recipe for crunchy dill pickles?

Lucille Cole, Oregon

There are several reasons that pickles become soft. Probably the most common is using cucumbers that are not very fresh. Pick your cukes just before making pickles. When you pick them and refrigerate them for several days or buy them at store, chances are high that your pickles will be soft. Another common cause of soft pickles is long processing time. Choose a recipe that has a maximum of 15 minutes total boiling time, and have your boiling water bath canner at a high simmer when you put the filled jars into it so they aren't sitting for a while in very hot water before starting to process them. Here is my favorite dill recipe from my book, *Growing and Canning Your Own Food.*

Quick dill spears:

1 gallon 4-inch fresh cucumbers
6 Tbsp. pickling salt
3 cups white vinegar
3 cups water
6 heads dill or ¾ cup dill seed
garlic (optional)

Rinse and remove blossom end, then cut cucumbers in half or quarters, lengthwise. Combine salt, vinegar, and water and bring to a boil. Pack cucumbers into hot jars. Mix in dill and garlic, if desired, with pickle spears. Leave ½ inch of headspace. Ladle boiling pickle brine over cucumbers, leaving ½ inch of headspace, covering cucumbers. Remove air bubbles. Wipe rim of jar clean; place hot, previously simmered lid on jar and screw down ring firmly tight. Process in a boiling water bath canner for 10 minutes.

You may also add mustard seed and a small, dried red pepper to make Polish or Kosher dills if you wish.

I use this recipe every year and my pickles are never soft. We like them with a crunch! Remember to serve refrigerated, which also helps keep the crunch in the pickles.

Virginia chunk sweet pickles

I'm looking for an old recipe. It's called Virginia Chunk Sweet Pickles. My mom made them for years, then I made them for years and now my daughter wants to make them and I have lost the recipe. We always put green food color in them to make them bright green. Nice at Christmas time.

Arlene Parkhurst

Not only have I heard of Virginia Chunk Sweet Pickles, but I have jars of them on my pantry shelves right now. They're good, crispy pickles, alright. Here's the recipe:

Virginia chunk sweet pickles:

Use 75 cukes (4-5 inches), or 2 gallons of smaller ones. Make a brine using 2 cups salt to one gallon of water. Boil the brine and pour it over cucumbers while it's still boiling hot. Weight down with a dish to keep the pickles under the brine. Let them stand one week, removing the scum daily. Then drain off the liquid and cut the cukes into chunks. For the next three mornings make a boiling solution of one gallon water and one tablespoon powdered alum and pour this over the drained pickles. (Make a fresh hot bath each morning.) On the fourth morning, drain and discard alum water. Heat 6 cups vinegar, 5 cups sugar, ⅓ cup pickling spice and 1 Tbsp. celery seed to boiling and pour over pickles. On the fifth morning drain this liquid off into a sauce pan and add 2 more cups of sugar to it, heat again to boiling and pour back over the pickles. On the sixth morning drain the liquid, add 1 more cup of sugar to it, heat it again to boiling, pack the pickles into sterilized jars and fill to within ½ inch of the top with the boiling liquid. Put on the caps and screw the bands firmly tight. Process the jars in a boiling water bath for 5 minutes. Yield: 18 pints.

Don't cheat and add all the sugar at once, or your pickles will shrivel.

Shriveled sweet pickles

I have a very good sweet pickle recipe (icicle pickles). They are very tasty and are always a big hit with everyone we serve them to. I do have a problem and I am wondering if you could help solve it for me. Some of the pickles get somewhat shriveled during the two weeks of processing them. Could it be the alum? I always keep them totally covered from the beginning stage of salt water throughout the final stages of pouring the hot syrup over them. They taste just fine but some of them just are not attractive for serving. What can I do different to prevent this problem?

Jeanne Ver Hage

Shriveling in pickles usually can be traced to four causes. The most common is using pickles that have been picked too far in advance of actual processing. Use very fresh cukes. Placing cucumbers in too strong a pickling or brine solution can cause shriveling, so always follow directions exactly. Using too sweet a pickling solution is my usual pickle-shriveler. This is why we usually increase the sugar slowly as the pickling process goes on. Shortcutting here by adding too much sugar really wrinkles those little gems quickly. I hope your pickles soon come out plump and smooth.

Sweet pickle relish

I would like to use some of the surplus cucumbers to make a relish. Do you have a recipe?

Wade Blevins, Arkansas

Sure, I have a recipe for cucumber relish. Several, in fact, but here's one of my favorites.

Sweet pickle relish:

8 medium cukes
4 medium onions
2 cups chopped green peppers
2 cups chopped red bell peppers
½ cup salt
7 cups sugar
4 cups vinegar
2 Tbsp. celery seed
2 Tbsp. mustard seed

Chop all vegetables and place in large bowl. Cover with salt and cold water. Let stand, covered, for two hours. Drain and rinse. Combine sugar, vinegar, and spices in a large pan and bring to a boil. Add drained vegetables and simmer for 10 minutes. Pack hot relish into hot pint or half-pint jars, leaving ¼ inch of headroom. Remove any air bubbles by running a hot knife down inside jar. Wipe the jar rim clean. Place a hot, previously boiled new lid on jar and screw down the ring firmly tight. Process in hot water bath for 10 minutes. Remove quickly and cool on folded dry towel. Do not overboil.

Sweet pickle chunks

Do you have a good recipe for sweet pickle chunks that doesn't involve soaking in brine solution? Something that can just be canned up quick? I'm overwhelmed with cukes this year.

Robin Balczewski, Washington

Most sweet pickles need to be soaked in iced salt brine before pickling to keep the crisp in the pickle. I scrub the cukes and cut them as needed, then brine them in ice water brine overnight so I can start the very next morning. Then I pick another batch in the afternoon to do the next day and so on. That way, I've always got a new batch all set to go and you really don't lose any time that way.

Repacking pickle relish

We buy pickle relish fairly cheap at the local Sam's Club in one-gallon plastic containers. I was wondering about repacking it in pint jars. Would any certain procedure have to be followed or could I just fill the jars, put the lids and rings on and store them?

Steve Dunn

Well, you could repack the relish in, say, sterilized pint jars and put a sterile lid on it and keep them in the fridge until all were used up. But I wouldn't just store them on the pantry shelf because they may go bad. There's no way to satisfactorily seal pickles of any type that have already been processed because in order to reseal them, you'd have to bring them to boiling and waterbath process them to seal the jars. This would make the relish very mushy. If I had room in the fridge, I'd keep repacked smaller jars in there, which would probably keep the relish nicer, longer. Of course, I'd rather make my own relish, as you'd guess. You miss half the fun if you don't put up your own food.

A head of fresh dill

I have a few pickle recipes that call for a "head of fresh dill." I was wondering what that is. Is it the entire sprig or half? I'm making dill pickles and the recipe isn't exact as to the head of dill.

Julie Argo

The "head" of dill is the entire seed head of a dill plant. But this can vary with the vitality of the plant. Generally a head of dill is about three to four inches in diameter, having a bounty of green seeds. Stronger dill flavor is had by using the same size head, with dried seeds. If your plants have smaller heads, simply use more of them. I often put one of these smaller heads on the bottom of the jar and another on top, with a small dried red pepper on top of that, for zing. Good pickling!

Brined dill pickles

I have been successfully fermenting sauerkraut just using canning salt and cabbage without a recipe. I tried fermenting cucumbers, but ended up with a slimy mess. I know there are many recipes using vinegar and cooking.

But, I remember my parents buying a pickle at a grocery store where they fished one out of just a wooden barrel full of brine. I remember they were crisp and tasty, with no vinegar taste. I would appreciate it if you could provide a recipe. By the way, I have found that one head of red cabbage in a bucket of green cabbage will turn the entire batch red (chopped up and fermenting of course).

Bernard Falkowski, Oregon

What you are referring to is brined dill pickles. But even these have vinegar; just not as much. To make brined dill pickles, you'll need (roughly):

10 lbs. cucumbers (4 to 6-inch)
6-8 bunches fresh dill
1½ cups canning salt
2 cups vinegar
2 gallons water
6 cloves garlic (optional)

Wash and drain cucumbers. Remove blossom end; leave ¼ inch of stem. Place a layer of dill in a clean crock. Add cucumbers to within 4 inches of the top. Combine salt, vinegar, and water; use pickling salt. Ladle over cucumbers. Place another layer of dill over the top and garlic, if desired. Weight cucumbers under the brine with a plate and a clean weight.

Store container in a cool place. Let cucumbers ferment until well-flavored and clear throughout. Check periodically for scum. If it forms, skim as necessary. Keep the pickles under the brine. You can home can the pickles in about 3 weeks. These pickles will usually keep in the crock until they are eaten. But if they are allowed exposure to the air, they will rot. So most folks go ahead and can them up. To do this, remove the pickles from the brine. Strain the brine and bring it to a boil in a large kettle. Pack the pickles into hot jars, leaving ½ inch of headroom. Ladle hot liquid over pickles, leaving ½ inch of headroom. Process in a boiling water bath for 15 minutes.

Soft and salty dill pickles

I tried for the first time to can dill pickles, and they came out soft and salty. How do I get them to come out crunchy? Is it the water or the processing in water bath? Please help.

Leona

Usually when pickles are salty, they have not been rinsed after soaking in salt water. Sometimes soft pickles come from high minerals in the water but most times it is from processing too long in the water bath. If your recipe calls for water bath processing, have your water at boiling when you are ready to place your jars into it. To keep cold jars from cracking, stand them in a sink full of quite warm water long enough for them to feel warm to the touch before placing them in the boiling water. Then get them in quickly and put the lid on. Count your time from when the kettle resumes a rolling boil. When the time is up, immediately remove the jars and place on a dry, folded towel with air circulation between the jars so they cool quickly. Keep out of drafts, though, or they might crack.

Do a small batch, using your recipe. If they turn out okay, great. You can check in a week. The pickles won't be real good, but you'll know if they are crisp and less salty. Place the opened jar in the fridge for a month, and let 'em cure longer so you don't waste them. If you still don't like the pickles, choose another recipe. There are dozens; some you like and some you don't … just like everything else.

Skim off the mold

I have filled a crock with cucumbers and the necessary vinegar and water and spices to make dill pickles. No mold has formed yet but my question is … how necessary is it to skim the mold from the top? After I got them made, it occurred to me that we might be gone on a 10 day trip before they are ready to can and the mold will form on top.

Laurel Roberts, Oregon

It is quite important to skim the mold from the top of the crock as the cucumbers pickle. If you don't, you risk the pickles picking up a moldy taste and possibly spoiling. Perhaps a friend or relative would be willing to come over to your house and skim your crock periodically if you must be gone. (I'd offer them a few jars of finished pickles as a bribe!)

Spices for pickles

First, I have to thank you for being so generous with your extensive knowledge of traditional and lower-tech ways of doing things.

My question is about pickles. I've been reading a lot of pickle recipes lately and they all seem to use similar spices (dill, mustard powder, etc.). I'd like to experiment, but wonder if other spices could cause problems in the pickling process — or maybe they are guaranteed to taste bad. Any advice?

Charles, Japan

Have at it, Charles! Experiment away. Just make sure to use the right amount of vegetables, salt, sugar, and vinegar, which are your pickling bases. The spices are just for flavoring and you can add or leave out what you want. Well, within reason, that is! When you make a new pickle, only make a few jars, to start. Then let them mellow a few weeks and open them to see what you've created. Some will be great, others so-so, but you'll probably be pleasantly surprised.

Canning sauerkraut

I know you make sauerkraut, but do you have a good but simple recipe for putting it in canning jars?

Judy Smith, Alabama

To can sauerkraut, just dip it out of the crock you brined it in and place it in a large kettle. Bring it to 185-210°F (just simmering, do not boil). Pack hot into hot jars, leaving ½ inch of headspace. Cover with hot liquid, leaving ½ inch of headspace. Remove any air bubbles. Wipe rim of jar clean; place hot, previously-simmered lid on the jar and screw down the ring firmly. Process pints for 15 minutes and quarts for 20 minutes in a boiling water bath canner.

Recipe for canning kraut

Do you know of or have any recipes for preparing home canned sauerkraut where you place shredded cabbage in canning jars and pour boiling water, sugar and salt mixture over cabbage to preserve without having to pack in churns, let sour and then process?

Avis & Linda Durham

There are several "non-crock" sauerkraut recipes. Here's one:

Quick and easy sauerkraut:

5 heads cabbage
pickling salt
white vinegar

Shred cabbage and fill the jars, packing down the cabbage snug but not tight. Pour boiling water over cabbage up to an inch from the top of the jar. Put 1 tsp. salt and 1 Tbsp. vinegar in each jar. Put on sterile lid and ring, screwing down firmly tight. Let ferment for 6 weeks. Then you may process in a boiling water bath canner for 25 minutes for quarts and 20 minutes for pints. If you live at an altitude over 1,000 feet, consult your canning manual for directions on increasing your processing time to suit your altitude.

Putting up sauerkraut

Do you have a good method of putting up sauerkraut? I did it years ago, but I don't seem to remember just how I did it. Thanks.

Andy Chumbley

One sauerkraut recipe I have that is very good is as follows:

50 lbs. cabbage
1 lb. canning salt

Clean the cabbage heads, removing any wilted, yellow, or dry leaves. Wash and drain the water off. Cut the cabbage into halves or quarters for ease of handling. Use a shredder or sharp knife on a cutting board and cut the cabbage into thin shreds.

In a large bowl or bucket, mix 3 Tbsp. salt and 5 lbs. of cabbage until it wilts. Remove and pack the salted shreds evenly into a large crock. Tamp it down well with your hands. Repeat until all cabbage is used. When done, juice will come to surface. If it doesn't, add a boiled, cool brine made of 2 Tbsp. salt to 1 quart of water.

The cabbage should fill the crock no more than 4 inches from the top. Cover the cabbage with a clean piece of an old white sheet, tucking the ends down along the sides of the crock. Place a china plate over cloth and cabbage, weighing it down to keep the cabbage under the brine constantly.

Set crock in an out-of-the-way place at room temperature.

Gas bubbles tell you the cabbage is fermenting. Skim off any scum each day. Be sure to reposition cloth and weighted plate.

The fermentation will be finished in 5 to 6 weeks. Treat your sauerkraut like livestock, tending carefully each day, and it will turn out perfectly.

You can home can the kraut by heating about 10 lbs. at a time to a simmer, not rolling boil. Then pack hot into hot quart jars leaving ½ inch of headspace. Cover with hot liquid, again leaving ½ inch of headspace. Wipe the rim, then place a boiled lid and ring on top, and screw the ring down firmly. Process the quarts for 20 minutes in a boiling water bath. Repeat until all kraut has been canned. The 50 pounds of cabbage will give you about 18 quarts of canned sauerkraut.

Keeping kraut lighter

How can I keep my cabbage from turning brown when canning kraut? I pack into jars, add salt, water, and let that ferment for about seven days then hot water bath. The kraut is always good but turns a little dark. I enjoy all of your articles and wonder how you have time to answer questions with such a busy lifestyle (living simple is not so simple).

T. Rose, West Virginia

Sauerkraut processed directly in the jars does tend to turn a little dark. It helps to keep the jars in a very dark place. Some folks even wrap the jars with newspaper to keep the light away. Kraut that is fermented in crocks, then canned is usually lighter in color.

Sometimes deadline comes too soon, I'll admit! Like this month, with me finishing up those nasty cancer treatments (the alternative didn't sound good to me, either), trying to get the new log house ready to move into before winter, and (finally) canning our garden like crazy. Sometimes I wish I were twins. Triplets?

Failed sauerkraut

In the January/February issue you described a recipe called the Florida quick method for making small amounts of sauerkraut. I followed the instructions to the letter but thought there should have been some brine added to the jars before leaving the 'kraut to ferment. What do I know? I wanted sauerkraut and did not want to fail in this endeavor. I put the jars in the basement with loose lids, forgot about them for a week, and then checked on them. My cabbage was black and smelled like the compost pile!

What went wrong? In order to recover from this culinary failure and assuage my bruised ego, I made pickled garlic from the March/April issue, which was a roaring success. I still have a hankering for homemade sauerkraut though.

Dan Ranger

Gee Dan, I'm sorry your kraut went belly up. But in any endeavor, this kind of thing happens while you're learning. I'll never forget my first attempt at cement work.

I think what happened is that you didn't pack the salted cabbage into the jars. In most canning instructions, "packing" simply means putting a food into the jars. With sauerkraut, "packing" means just that. You must just about pound the cabbage down into the container. This releases air pockets and also helps make the juice flow that mixes with the salt to become the brine in which the cabbage ferments. Another thing to watch for is to make sure that all the cabbage is packed below the juice/brine.

Tomato pickles

I am looking for a recipe for pickled whole little green tomatoes, I have your cookbook and other books and the only thing I found has sugar in it. The ones I have had are more on the order of pickled okra (pepper, garlic, salt, and vinegar). Do you have a recipe to share?

Cindy Adams, Alabama

Tomato pickles:

1 gallon small green tomatoes
1½ Tbsp. salt
2-3 cloves garlic, peeled
3 cups water
4 cups vinegar
dill (optional)

Add salt and garlic to vinegar and water and simmer 15 minutes. Pack tomatoes into hot, sterilized jars, leaving 1 inch of headspace. Add a head of dill to top, if desired. Ladle boiling pickling solution over tomatoes, leaving 1 inch of headspace. Remove air bubbles. Process pints for 30 minutes in a boiling water bath canner. If you live at an altitude above 1,000 feet, consult your canning book for instructions in adjusting your processing time to suit your altitude.

Pickling banana peppers

I am new at canning and last summer I grew some banana peppers and tried pickling them, but every jar I tried to pickle came out slimy, chewy, and bitter-tasting. I even tried cooking them first and adding alum, but each time they were slimy. What did I do wrong? Help!

Stephanie Cruz, Kansas

Boy, Stephanie, I've canned tons of peppers of all kinds, and have never had slimy or bitter ones. Try this and see if yours turn out fine next time.

Cut two small slits in each pepper. This lets the pickling solution reach all parts of the pepper. Mix 1½ cups salt with 4 quarts of ice water and pour over a gallon of freshly picked peppers with slits cut. Weight the peppers down with a china plate and let stand overnight in a cool place. Drain and rinse thoroughly. Combine: 2 cups water, ¼ cup sugar, 2½ quarts vinegar. Bring to a boil. Pack peppers into a hot jar and pour boiling pickling solution over the peppers to ½ inch of the top of the jar. Remove any air bubbles. Wipe rim clean. Place hot, previously simmered lid on jar and screw down ring firmly tight. Process pints for 10 minutes in a boiling water bath canner, making sure to count from the time the water returns to a full boil after adding the jars.

Pickling garlic

I am looking for a good recipe to pickle garlic. I have searched my canning books and there isn't one recipe in any of them.

Becky Adams, Arkansas

Simply peel the individual cloves of garlic, then soak them overnight in a brine of ½ cup salt to a gallon of cold water. Weigh down the cloves so they remain under the brine. In the morning, rinse the cloves well with fresh water. To four quarts of garlic cloves, you will need 8 cups white vinegar, 2 cups sugar, and ¼ cup pickling spices (optional). Tie pickling spices in a cloth bag and add to vinegar and sugar in a large pot. Bring to a boil and simmer 10 minutes.

Pack garlic cloves in sterilized, hot pint jars to within an inch of the top. Remove spice bag from simmering pot and pour boiling syrup over garlic cloves, filling to within ½ inch of top of jar. Wipe jar rim and place hot, previously boiled new jar lid on jar and tighten ring down firmly tight. Process in hot water bath for 10 minutes. If you like hotter garlic, you may add one or two dried hot peppers to each jar before putting the boiling syrup on.

Pickled garlic turning dark

I pickled garlic recently and several of the cloves turned a blue/green. I was told that they were perfectly okay to eat and in fact they were. However, it doesn't look very nice and I am wondering how to pickle garlic without the cloves turning dark or blue/green.

Susan Fleming

If it was just the top layer of the pickled garlic that turned unappetizing blue green, I'd suspect that they touched the lids. Simply fill the jars less full with cloves of garlic and pickling solution.

If the color persisted throughout the jar, I'd suspect one of these: minerals (especially iron) in the water or iron cooking utensils, perhaps a cast iron pot in which the garlic and pickling solution was heated in, or perhaps spices and vinegar reacting to the garlic. If it is minerals in the water, simply use water without iron (filtered or bottled) for your garlic pickling. It really makes a difference sometimes.

Pickled walnuts

I am in need of a pickled walnut recipe. My family's "1800" Worcestershire sauce recipe calls for "pickled walnuts" and I've had to leave it out all these years because it can't be found. In your #86 issue on preparing black walnuts, to can them do you cover the nuts with water, vinegar, or nothing at all?

Name withheld

I do not have a recipe for pickled walnuts, but you can pickle just about anything by simply immersing it in vinegar. If it were me, I'd simply toss a handful of walnuts into a half-pint jar and cover them with vinegar. Put on the lid and store in the fridge for a week or two. That will give you "pickled walnuts."

Pickled red beet eggs

Can you please tell me how to can red beet eggs?

Lana S.

I think what you're looking for is a recipe for pickled red beet dyed hard boiled eggs. Here is a recipe.

Pickled red beet eggs:

6 cups strongly colored beet juice made from boiling sliced beets in water

3 cups sugar

6 cups vinegar

1 tsp. salt

36 peeled hard boiled eggs

Mix the first four ingredients and bring to a boil and hold there for five minutes, stirring constantly. Pour over 36 peeled, hard boiled eggs and refrigerate, tightly covered for 24 hours. Dip out the eggs and pack into sterilized jars. Bring the vinegar solution to a boil and pour over the eggs to within ½ an inch of the jar's top. Wipe rim of jar clean and place a hot, previously boiled lid on, screwing the ring down firmly tight. Process in boiling water bath for 20 minutes.

Canning pickled fish

My mother is 87 and still cans everything she can get her hands on, from beans to beaver. She also pickles fish, but for long-term storage the fish is either smoked or salted. How can the pickled fish be canned to last as long as the bought pickled herring, pork hocks, or pigs' feet which we have stored for quite some time?

Dale Jacobs, Alaska

Sorry, but canning pickled fish at home can result in an off-colored, sometimes bitter end-product.

Other books available from *Backwoods Home Magazine*

- The Best of the First Two Years
- A Backwoods Home Anthology—The Third Year
- A Backwoods Home Anthology—The Fourth Year
- A Backwoods Home Anthology—The Fifth Year
- A Backwoods Home Anthology—The Sixth Year
- A Backwoods Home Anthology—The Seventh Year
- A Backwoods Home Anthology—The Eighth Year
- A Backwoods Home Anthology—The Ninth Year
- A Backwoods Home Anthology—The Tenth Year
- A Backwoods Home Anthology—The Eleventh Year
- A Backwoods Home Anthology—The Twelfth Year
- A Backwoods Home Anthology—The Thirteenth Year
- A Backwoods Home Anthology—The Fourteenth Year
- A Backwoods Home Anthology—The Fifteenth Year
- A Backwoods Home Anthology—The Sixteenth Year
- A Backwoods Home Anthology—The Seventeenth Year
- A Backwoods Home Anthology—The Eighteenth Year
- A Backwoods Home Anthology—The Nineteenth Year
- Emergency Preparedness and Survival Guide
- Backwoods Home Cooking
- Can America Be Saved From Stupid People
- The Coming American Dictatorship, Parts I-XI
- Chickens: a beginner's handbook
- Starting Over: Chronicles of a Self-Reliant Woman
- Dairy goats: a beginner's handbook
- Self-Reliance: Recession-proof your pantry
- Making a Living: creating your own job
- Harvesting the Wild: gathering & using food from nature
- Hardyville Tales
- Growing and Canning Your Own Food
- Jackie Clay's Pantry Cookbook

You'll want all eight books in this great Ask Jackie series:

- ❃ Animals
- ❃ Canning Basics
- ❃ Food Storage
- ❃ Gardening
- ❃ Homestead Cooking
- ❃ Homesteading
- ❃ Pressure Canning
- ❃ Water Bath Canning

About the author

Jackie is a lifelong homesteader. From the tender age of three, she dreamed of having her own land, complete with chickens and horses. Learning life skills such as canning, gardening, and carpentry from her mother, father, and grandmother, she slowly became a very experienced homesteader. She has more than 45 years of experience foraging wild foods, growing a garden, raising homestead animals such as goats, cattle, horses, pigs, and, of course, chickens. Jackie cans hundreds of jars of gourmet-quality, homegrown food every single year. The family eats like kings!

She lives on a wilderness 120-acre homestead with her husband, Will (also a lifelong homesteader), and son, David. They raise nearly 90% of their own food and as much as possible, strive for a more self-reliant lifestyle while living off-grid.

Jackie has written for many years for *Backwoods Home Magazine*, doing both feature articles on all aspects of low-tech homesteading as well as the informative Ask Jackie column since 1999. She also maintains a popular "Ask Jackie" blog at the magazine's website, www.backwoodshome.com/blogs/JackieClay. She has also written several books including *Growing and Canning Your Own Food, Jackie Clay's Pantry Cookbook,* and *Starting Over,* as well as several more on animal care.